Alone

Coping with the Loss of a Partner

Splendid
PUBLICATIONS

Alone Again

Coping with the Loss of a Partner

Dawn Cawley

Splendid
PUBLICATIONS

Alone Again
Coping with the Loss of a Partner

Splendid
PUBLICATIONS

Unit 7,
Twin Bridges Business Park
South Croydon
Surrey CR2 6PL

www.splendidpublications.co.uk

British Library Cataloguing in Publication Data is available from The British Library.

ISBN 978-1-909109-75-9

Commissioning Editor: Shoba Vazirani

Designed by Swerve Creative Design & Marketing
www.swerve-creative.co.uk

Printed and bound by CPI Group (UK) Ltd, Croydon, CR0 4YY

About the Author

It is more than four years since my husband Alan died.

He was diagnosed with prostate cancer which spread to the bones and eventually to his brain. Alan passed away in hospital three years later aged seventy-one.

The purpose of this book is not to dwell on those days leading up to his death. There were many good times during the period before then and I am convinced he always clung to the hope of returning to good health. This is more about the process of moving on after losing your life partner.

'Why has she suddenly decided to write this book?' I hear you say.

A life-long friend suddenly and unexpectedly found

himself in a similar situation and it led me to retrace my steps along the path while thinking I might be in a position to help him. We have an ageing population and I know there must be many others in a similar situation; that's the reason I have decided to put pen to paper.

I hope my experiences will offer solace to others who find themselves alone again after losing their beloved partner. Whether you've shared decades of happy marriage or have been in a relationship for just a short while. Whether you're in the twilight of your life or a mere youngster with decades ahead of you, losing your 'other half' is one of the worst ordeals you will experience but please know, there is help available out there to get you through the dark days ahead. I'm not promising to offer you all the answers here, but I have been where you now find yourself, so I can hopefully offer you some.

****

Contents

Alone Again

Introduction

Nothing can ever prepare you for being on your own after the death of a partner. Often it has been a long and happy marriage and the surviving partner feels devastated and lost. Perhaps it has been a short union with future plans shattered. Or a long relationship filled with ups and downs, children, grandchildren and shared history… the initial reaction is the same: pain and disbelief.

Even if your partner was terminally ill and you'd had your chance to say your goodbyes, it's still a shock when it happens. Nobody truly understands that awful, desolate feeling unless they've been in the same situation.

When Alan passed away, my grown-up son and daughter, both with a couple of children of their own, helped me in different ways, visiting their Dad at home and later in hospital when he was very ill. Amanda was an amazing source of strength and comfort to me during those grim days leading up to Alan's death, and later my son Russ took over the arrangements: steering me in the right direction and making sure all the formalities were taken care of. Although grieving themselves, they explained everything to the grandchildren and helped by 'phoning close friends.

I couldn't cope with a big, public funeral so instead we organised a private cremation with immediate family only, followed by a moving church service. It was purely my decision and I was apprehensive about family reaction when I suggested it, but everyone was very much in favour. We were all satisfied with the arrangements and spent a lot of time discussing details to make sure Alan's send-off was the way we wanted it. And the way we knew he would have wanted it. It gave us the opportunity to say goodbye and fall apart as a family, without causing embarrassment to ourselves and others. We had breathing space and a chance to get our act together before facing everyone.

After the ordeal of the cremation we returned home for a stiff drink and checked everything was ready before going to the church.

There was a huge sense of relief once the service was over and I was then able to relax, meeting and greeting friends and relations, knowing that they knew and understood – no explanations necessary.

****

Alone Again

Reality

There is no right or wrong way to cope with the days ahead. Every person and their circumstances are different. Some folk begin the grieving process while their partners are still alive. Perhaps they accept that the illness is terminal and they have had time to become accustomed to the inevitable, unlike those who are suddenly and unexpectedly bereaved.

Is it worse to witness a loved one's daily deterioration, often with little quality of life and no hope, or to be parted without warning? Either way is devastating and most of the time, we aren't given a choice.

I managed to cope when people treated me with a 'business as usual,' approach, but when some showed sympathy and were kind to me, it could lead to tears. I made a point of saying, "Don't be nice to me, I can't take it." I felt honesty was the best policy but I appreciate you might be different and may find comfort in a sympathetic hug.

We hear about the various stages of grieving, ie shock and devastation: "It can't be true." Anger: "It's not fair, he/she didn't deserve it." Guilt: "Could I have done more?" Panic: "How am I going to manage alone?"

There is no set pattern. People react in many ways and it is often unpredictable.

Loneliness is the greatest problem. You've shared a life with someone, probably for a long time and now you are alone and you are simply not prepared for the dramatic change. Hopefully, within these pages there are a few tips to help you through this distressing time.

Like so many others, I find the worst time of the day is the evening, when you return to an empty house. No point in shouting, "Hi, I'm back!" or waiting for the familiar, "How was it?" There is nobody to answer and that's desperately sad, especially at first. How often in the past have you come home to discover your partner engrossed in a TV programme, and thought, I don't think he/she even noticed that I'm back and felt miffed? Now that presence has gone. It's just you, and that's the way it will be for the foreseeable future, maybe always.

These days, even though on many occasions I've resolved to go to bed early, it never seems to happen. I'm either watching something trivial on TV, or faffing around. There's nobody to chivvy me with, "It's time we hit the sack," or, "Look at that clock, it's bedtime!"

Mornings can be equally daunting. Insomnia might affect some, but, assuming that you have had a good night's sleep, you will miss the familiar early morning remark, "You were snoring for England last night," or "What shall we do today?" You have the task of getting up and facing the day ahead on your own and loneliness is one of the biggest challenges you're likely to face.

****

Perhaps this might help…

One of my greatest buddies is the radio. The first thing I do every morning is switch it on and shatter the quietness that surrounds me. It helps listening to music, or maybe shouting, "Rubbish!" at some politician pontificating on Radio 4. The radio is less trouble than a dog, although you might consider getting a four-footed friend if it fits into your lifestyle.

At least a radio doesn't demand 'walkies' when it's pouring with rain outside. Neither do you have to feed it at inconvenient times, or have to let it out to do its business late at night. Fido would certainly be a loyal companion and I know many people who've found a new lease of life after getting a furry friend, but it's only fair to an animal if you are prepared to give it the attention it deserves.

A light here and there and the radio (here we go, the radio again) switched on before going out makes your home a more inviting place to return alone after a day out. When you put the key in the door it is no longer completely quiet and somehow feels more welcoming. Too much silence can be depressing and it is important to avoid falling into this trap.

I'm very fortunate as I have been blessed with a

loving family and many good friends, but there is no denying that there are lonely days, or as I prefer to call them, days on my own.

I think it's unfair to impose on the family too much if I can help it. They have their own busy lives to lead. It's lovely seeing them, but I'd hate to think they thought it was their duty to entertain me all the time and the 'old woman' was becoming a nuisance: a bit like a dose of cod liver oil – not much fun, but required.

Another good 'friend' is the telephone. If you haven't spoken to anybody for sometime and you are feeling low, a familiar voice can work wonders. There is a lot of truth in that well-known saying, 'phone a friend.' I think women tend to ring friends for a chat more often than men, which is a shame - it's good to make and receive calls. On the other hand if things are really bad and you would just like to hear a voice, any voice, the telephone directory can offer many services that you could contact, eg the cinema for film times. You can't chat to a person, but at least it's a friendly voice, and you might even be persuaded to view a current film.

In the local paper or *Saga* magazine it is easy to find an advertisement from a lonely person with a telephone number. It can be interesting just to listen without acting upon it, but beware, don't get too carried away, for it could result in a hefty 'phone bill. I refuse to admit or deny having tried this out!

The family, apart from mourning a parent, will be concerned about you, and how you are coping. The roles are reversed and they are taking care of you now. If you appear inconsolable it won't help, and only adds to their worries and makes them feel inadequate. They might feel guilty that they can't make everything right for you, even though they know it would be impossible. You can never put the clock back. Distance might concern them, "If only we lived nearer..."

I feel everyone owes it to their family and friends to make an effort and prove that they are managing, even if it is a struggle. There are many things that can be kept private without letting them realise how hard it can be. Not everyone can act convincingly, but at least they can have a darned good try. No need to tell them about, to quote Cliff Richard, 'Those lonely nights.' They know it's tough, and are aware of what you are going through without also having to endure the painful details. In your pain and grief, try not to forget that they're grieving also and have to be allowed the time and space to work through their emotions, just like you.

By all means talk to them and mention your feelings, but also prove that you are trying to overcome them and making an effort, difficult though it may be. They'll admire your progress and achievement. I am not suggesting the stiff upper lip method right away, for it is often essential to be able to unburden yourself to family or close friends in the early days. It would be dangerous if suppressed emotions built up inside. Grief needs an outlet otherwise it might eventually cause the river to burst its banks. It is necessary to let it all out in order to move forward.

Moving ahead is important, and can be especially difficult if you have lost a dominant partner who was in charge and tended to organise many things such as the family finances. If you haven't family or an understanding friend to go to for practical advice and you are unable to cope, there are places where you can get help. It shows strength, not weakness, to admit that you need guidance and have the courage to seek it.

Perhaps this might help...

Sometimes it is easier to talk to a stranger or a counsellor, who will encourage you to face a future on your own.

For some who find it impossible to cope, a GP is usually the first port of call, especially if health is being affected. He may mention a bereavement society to help with the grieving process, or suggest counselling, which would require a doctor's referral.

There is absolutely no shame in seeking the help of a professional if needed, especially when there are no family members available. A bereaved person might not wish to burden their family, or perhaps they are estranged. They might be completely alone and friendless. Let's face it, the older we get, the more likely this is to be the case.

Isolation can be the cause of depression, but help is always close at hand. If a word with the doctor or a vicar/priest is out of the question, the library and the telephone book is a useful source of information.

The Samaritans are available at any time and most of their calls are not from the suicidal, more often from a lonely person who needs to hear a kind voice and know there is someone there for them.

****

Aftermath

Within a short space of time after a death, the deceased's Will has to be read and the finances sorted and generally a visit to the bank is necessary.

Perhaps your partner was an organised person and left instructions that he/she wanted carried out. Sadly this is not always the case and it can be chaos, especially when no Will is forthcoming.

How often have we heard of family feuds caused over a Will? What is to be done with the personal effects? Who has what? It can be a minefield!

Perhaps there are trustees and possibly a solicitor is involved in probate. Obtaining probate is a system whereby Wills are validated by the High Court of Justice.

A Will almost invariably bears the name/s of the executor/s whose job it is to fulfil the wishes of the deceased, but the absence of named executors does not invalidate the Will. There is a legal process for getting new executors appointed. An executor can also be a beneficiary and in many cases fulfils both roles.

The executor/s are obliged to swear an oath in front of a solicitor/court regarding the Will, the date the deceased died and a promise to carry out the terms as stipulated in the Will.

A probate fee, decided by the government, is paid and the Will is then submitted through one of the many registries in the country (many large towns have a registry).

After approximately three weeks, the probate court issues 'probate,' which is a single sheet of paper, along with a copy of the Will, stating the date when the deceased died and naming the executor/s.

The original Will is kept at the probate department and official copies can be obtained from the court, currently at a cost of £1 each and are as valid as the original.

The executor/s can now proceed to collect the assets, pay the debts (which include reasonable funeral expenses) and distribute total assets ('net') to the beneficiaries.

At all times it is necessary to produce a copy of probate and the Will, except in the case of items which can be delivered by hand.

Gordon Bowley LLB has written a book called *Probate*, which might prove useful in managing the legal and financial aspects of death.

For a fee a solicitor or a bank can be involved. Sorting out a Will and its personal effects can prove to be a minefield, especially as feelings will be running high. As mentioned before, family rifts often occur because of a Will. Seeking professional help might prevent this happening, and hopefully keep things in proportion and on an even keel, but it will take time.

If the executor/s are dead, the beneficiaries apply to court for a suitable substitute. A Will does not fail through lack of an executor.

If there is no Will the same process applies with the official document named Letters of Administration. The law lays down detailed rules as to how the monies will be distributed.

Distant relations are sought and if there is no Will and no apparent beneficiaries, the money automatically goes to the Government to reduce national debt.

Even without family, it is always advisable to leave a Will. Instead of the State benefiting, a deceased person may have preferred their money to go to friends or a favourite charity, but unfortunately without a Will, this wish will remain unfulfilled.

***

Personal effects include finances, jewellery, clothes, property and contents, photographs and documents and so on and will involve the surviving partner. This can be difficult. When do you start sorting through personal effects? Like so many things, it's completely up to you.

Everybody is different and you need to listen to yourself and know when you are ready and it is the right time. Don't let anyone tell you it's 'time to move on' if you can't face going through your late husband's suits or your late wife's jewellery.

Dealing and coping with bereavement is a very personal journey and some people take years to get around to looking through their beloved's things, while others prefer not to be constantly reminded of their loss and begin clearing away belongings almost immediately. There is no rule here.

Being busy sorting everything might be an escape, but it can be harrowing, "He loved that baseball cap," "She bought that skirt while we were on holiday last year." Hopefully, in time, those memories will cease to hurt as much and might even raise a fond smile.

It's depressing having to turn out a deceased person's clothing and personal treasures and it can be sad parting with favourite items. As I say, a wardrobe can remain untouched for years, sometimes forever. It may bring back too many memories of a loved one. There is no right or wrong here.

Aftermath

Only a short time ago, while turning out an old chest, I discovered a pair of my husband's shorts and a tee-shirt which momentarily threw me, but now I've got used to seeing the address book full of his handwriting.

I found that I gradually got around to sorting out Alan's clothes. Russ was given his leather jacket which fitted him well. He also had his Dad's watch as I know that was what Alan would have wanted. Amanda was warned that she would have to wait her turn until I depart! She'll be disappointed about the shoes. I wear a size four and she needs a size six.

***

Being pleasantly occupied is important. If you have family and friends, this will be the time when they rally around, with invitations for meals, or suggest trips, maybe a coffee somewhere. Do take advantage of these offers. I know a widower who

admits that he never turns down an invitation.
Good for him!

I found my diary was hectic for the first four to
six months, and it helped no end. As time went
on, the invitations slowed down, giving me the
opportunity to assess my new situation and to
pursue hobbies and interests of my own. I went
OTT with everything: possibly as a blanking out
process.

Apart from meeting friends and going out,
all the stuff I'd placed on the back burner
during Alan's illness came to the fore again: the
entertainment group, choir, hospital radio, and
writing. The answerphone was inundated with
messages from the family, wondering where I was,
"We can't get hold of you - you're always out!"

If I found a blank page, I'd fill it! I had an
obsession about time running out and resolved
to do everything while I was able. Hopefully I've

calmed down now and am acting a little more sensibly, although some might disagree.

It sometimes takes time for some people to regain their sense of humour. Don't bury it with your partner – they wouldn't have wanted that!

A fellow who lives down the road couldn't adjust for ages. Although he had the support of family, friends and neighbours, he insisted on visiting his wife's grave daily and was unable to part with any of her belongings. Friends became worried, but slowly the visits became less frequent and he began to realise that life had to go on without her. He needed to come to terms with her death in his own time.

Another of my friends lost her husband to Alzheimer's disease. It was a long, debilitating illness and she admitted that she had no guilt, only relief when he passed away. At last he was at peace, free from pain and suffering. It was also her turn to restart her life and after years of taking care of him, she deserved her newly acquired freedom.

Gradually you adapt to change, and it's a good idea to structure life by planning the days and weeks ahead. There are always everyday household tasks: cleaning, shopping, washing, ironing and so on, which have to be done but it helps to plan a variety of things on different days to make life more interesting. Occasionally give yourself a treat.

I find that I am eating out more frequently. We have a network of cronies (more of that later) who enjoy dining in various restaurants and hostelries; this unfortunately is not helpful weight-wise!

Generally we fit into the 'Ladies who lunch' category, but it's not always a lunchtime meal, and a lonely, starving gentleman is always welcome to join us.

***

Aftermath

After a bereavement, many are affected with disturbed sleep and eating patterns. Try to organise a routine. It's not a good idea to eat only when you think or feel like it or to skip a meal altogether. Maybe you are not hungry, or just can't be bothered (cooking for one can be boring). Make a point of eating at a certain time, even if it's only a snack. Everyone owes it to their family and friends to remain as healthy as possible with a sensible diet and lifestyle.

As mentioned before, I still foolishly mess around when it's bedtime, watching TV, a video or something on iPlayer. Perhaps I discovered a programme recorded long ago that hasn't been deleted and looks inviting.

Another distraction is reading the newspaper or a book instead of thinking about settling down for the night. Not a good idea, but it's my choice and I've only myself to blame if I can't sleep properly or wake up late the following day. It's something I'm looking to improve upon going forward.

On a Sunday night I have to remember to put out the wheelie bin, which was always my husband's job. On many occasions I have trundled it down the drive wearing a thick coat over my nightdress, keeping my fingers crossed that nobody sees me.

Some people are able to cope sooner than others. Maybe they have had a helping hand from their partner before departure. A friend from choir was told that her husband had terminal cancer. When they came to terms with the news, he insisted that he taught her all the important things she would need to know when left on her own. He taught her what to do in an emergency, eg when the electricity suddenly went off, how to mend a fuse and change a tyre and so on and how to deal with financial matters. When he became very ill they bought a notebook and he wrote down a list of instructions. At the end of his life he told her that he thought it was time he went into a hospice nearby, which he did. He died the following day. She was lucky that she had such a caring and pragmatic husband and after he'd gone, she was able to cope far better than many others who didn't know where to begin when it came to fending for themselves.

A kick up the backside can be a good thing. I was taught a lesson a while ago when I did something stupid. One morning, before I was dressed, for some unknown reason, I suddenly got the urge to hand wash a favourite top. The sun was shining and I ventured into the garden wearing a pair of backless slippers. The garment dripped water ahead of me, and yours truly slipped on a step and landed face down on the concrete.

Alone Again

I lay there for a while, feeling sorry for myself
and aware that there was nobody to help me up
or console me. After pulling myself together, I
stumbled, still shaking, into the bathroom, where
I sat on the toilet, and applied a wet flannel to the
wounds.

On seeing the family later that day, I received
a right royal roasting, which was unnecessary.
By then I realised I had been foolish. A tough
lesson to learn, but it taught me to consider the
repercussions. It could have resulted in a broken
arm or leg, possibly worse, and I could have
remained there for ages until someone found
me. Nowadays I catch hold of the banisters when
coming downstairs, and choose not to go out if it's
icy, especially with a wet, dripping garment!

****

Getting out and about

Some find it difficult leaving the house after the death of their partner. They dread meeting people, and some of the people that they do meet, don't know how to deal with the situation. I've heard instances when a person has deliberately crossed the road in order not to come into contact with a recently bereaved friend or acquaintance. They might pretend not to see you, while thinking, "Should I mention anything about his/her partner." They don't intend to be unsympathetic, but they are unsure what to do.

On the other hand there are those who are so sympathetic that you are reduced to tears immediately, and everybody is embarrassed. One of my dearest friends offered sympathy by saying I was being brave and it must be difficult for me, which completely finished me off! I told everyone to treat me as usual and not to be extra nice to me.

It's probably best to be straightforward and admit to the bereaved that you've heard their sad news and don't really know what to say. They will probably be grateful that they don't have to go into painful details and explanations. They might just appreciate a "Hello, nice to see you out and about again," and then it's easy to talk about other things.

Some widows and widowers are unable to function for many months, due to their grief. It is necessary to take this into account if they don't turn up at familiar places like church, or art class.

Everyone has to be allowed to come to terms with their loss in their own way but do keep a careful watch on someone you know who's in this position and if it's you, please try not to hide away for too long. It's too easy to become reclusive and allow your thoughts to dwell entirely on your loss and wallow in sadness, but it's no good moping around the house. You have to help yourself.

It's better to make an effort to go out, or, if at home, find a distraction when things begin to get to you, perhaps the TV, an exciting book, or a hobby to help distract you from sad thoughts.

***

If the family live away, they might well invite the remaining parent to spend time with them after the funeral. Sometimes, this can lead to a permanent arrangement which can prove to be a lifeline. But sadly, in this day and age when everyone's busy working long hours and maybe room is at a premium, this is becoming less common. A short stay with a son or daughter after the funeral can be a welcome break, but there is still the daunting problem of returning home.

There are inevitable adjustments and changes to be made. You may decide to move house - often to be nearer family or to downsize. This is a big decision, and not one to be taken lightly, as you are vulnerable early on and may not be thinking clearly. There is much to consider, so don't rush it; you could regret it later. Time for careful consideration is essential before embarking on anything that is so important. I've learned that the bereaved should take at least a year if possible, to make any long-term plans, particularly moving house.

It was not a decision I had to make, as both my son and daughter live quite near, but I can understand that the idea might appeal to someone left alone, particularly if they have no friends or interests in the area. They could go away and make new friends and interests while having their family close by. It could be the start of a new life.

Staying in the same home can work, with several breaks so you can enjoy weekends and time with family, but getting back to catch up with friends and neighbours is a great incentive.

Normally the 'moving on' process occurs gradually and naturally as you work through grieving, so whatever you decide to do, it is important to occupy the mind in order that the 'moving on' process can proceed. Find a project.

The church can be a source of comfort to many. Apart from the religious aspect, you may meet and make new friends. It's up to you how involved you become. The church would benefit from your contribution and input and you may enjoy the fellowship in return. Religion offers solace in many ways during difficult and traumatic times so don't dismiss it out of hand if you're struggling, yet don't consider yourself a 'believer'.

There are also societies and clubs that welcome new members and often there is a committee place to be filled. It is another source of involvement if you have time and interest. I know of a friend who joined a rock choir after losing her other half. She found it both welcoming and uplifting singing her heart out each week and two years on, has made some solid new friendships.

Winter is more depressing than the summer months. The days are shorter and there is less opportunity to get out and about. Some enjoy the prospect of a cosy room with an inviting fire – many don't. Weather can affect people and there are those who can't wait for spring to arrive so they can admire the new green leaves, fresh blossom and colourful flowers. Perhaps working in their own garden, is their favourite hobby.

Walking appeals to some, (it's not limited to any particular season, of course). It's a good form of exercise, providing you are fit and able.

Voluntary work can be rewarding, and there is so much to choose from. The local library can supply information, and they will also have an impressive list of day and evening classes, which could be of interest and while away the time, especially during the winter. Hospitals are always looking for volunteers to chat to the elderly who are often left on wards with no one to visit them. How rewarding to be able to brighten up someone's day just by popping in to say hello?

The local paper is also a useful source of information. Why not look up what's going on and get involved somehow? Maybe attend a meeting and have your say about the development of your area, or take up a cause, perhaps send a letter to the 'post box page'? Writing can be therapeutic, and who knows, you might produce an unexpected best seller once you get going!

One of my widowed friends has become engrossed in her family tree. She has traced and met many previously unknown relatives which has given her a whole new lease of life and much excitement. It's taken her months and months and proved to be a good distraction from her grief and loneliness.

Another one-eyed monster has taken over society these days – the computer. With modern technology, encouragement from the clever clogs, and the embarrassing knowledge of the very young, especially grandchildren, it can be most disconcerting, especially as I've only recently mastered the potato peeler! Many are hooked by the computer, which is great, when they produce inspirational work. It can be a lifeline, especially if you find it difficult to get out into the fresh air. Friends of mine have opened up Facebook accounts and now happily keep in touch with long lost relatives and acquaintances across the globe from the comfort of their sofas! Or they use their tablets to skype friends and grandchildren as they go about their busy lives. What a wonderful way of keeping loved ones close.

****

Alone Again

Realisation

There are unfamiliar emotions that rise to the surface and often overtake you after the death of a partner: grief, guilt, blame and possibly bitterness in the main. There are various stages of grief and many unanswered questions spring to mind. Is it a punishment? Why did someone else recover and not my partner? If only…? Perhaps…? Maybe if the Dr/hospital …? Why me? Why us?

Perhaps there is envy of those still in a long-term relationship? It's normal to feel this way but remember, they too one day will have to face what you're experiencing now.

Endless thoughts haunt the mind continually and there are never satisfactory answers. Even if there were, it wouldn't change anything. Nothing can be done to alter the present situation and you are only torturing yourself.

Early days usually consist of the slow gradual process of picking up the threads, and facing a different and changed way of living, but there has to be a time for acceptance. If you never learn to let go, it could ruin the rest of your life. Easier said than done as life will never be the same, but an effort has to be made to create a fulfilling future. It's what your partner would have wanted for you and you for them had the situation been reversed.

Family and friends will be there to help and give encouragement, but they have their own commitments. Fulfilment can only be achieved by one person – that's you.

This may be difficult to comprehend now, but it is important to think of other people, yes even at this painful time. How am I affecting them? If it's someone 'in the same boat,' they will understand, but when they haven't 'been there,' how can they possibly relate in the same way as someone who has? Adjustment takes time. People who are close want the best for you. They are understanding and will make allowances, but if they come to the conclusion that you are accepting their kindness without making any sort of effort, they will eventually lose patience and you risk losing their on-going support.

When you enjoy the company of others, in return you have to make sure they enjoy yours. I would hate to think that I had visited friends, and after spending time with me, they were relieved to see the back of me. For the sake of their friendship

Alone Again

I vowed never to inflict my sadness on them or burden them. I cry privately and alone.

When you have a good time, never feel guilty about it. Try to think of it as enjoying yourself for both of you. Often I've seen a film or been to the theatre or a concert, and thought how much my husband would have loved it. Bitter-sweet thoughts.

***

There are occasions in the early days when the pain of loss is so great, that the bereaved person sobs uncontrollably, both men and women, but generally it is done in private. Some are unable to function properly, finding the simplest things impossible to deal with; there are so many memories surrounding them and everything is a constant reminder of their partner. Hopefully, with time, life will become less difficult. It's frightening having to deal with bills and problems when you have never had the responsibility before.

Marriages are made in heaven, but only if it's a union between two saints. Very few can honestly say that they've always agreed on everything, never had a cross word, and life has been a complete bed of roses. Have any of us had a totally perfect life?

We were friendly with one particular couple, and enjoyed many entertaining evenings with them. They both had strong opinions on various subjects and frequently disagreed. Time spent with them was never boring. We would often hear, "Don't be ridiculous, Fenella." (not her real name) and her reply, "You obviously weren't paying attention, Oswald."

There was never anything malicious in their relationship and it never got out of hand. They were happily married for over forty years.

I attended his funeral recently, and no, she was not responsible for manslaughter. Sadly he died of ill health, and I know for sure how much she will miss him and their arguments and banter.

Some couples are so devoted that they have no separate hobbies and do everything together. Different interests can enhance a marriage by giving them both food for thought and conversation. Without separate involvement, if one partner dies, the other will be completely lost, with nothing to fall back on or to interest them. If this is the position in which you find yourself now, I am sorry as I know how especially difficult it will be for you to venture out alone. However, I also know that this next chapter in your life is an opportunity to try new things and to forge a different kind of future for yourself.

***

Nobody can know their offspring better than a partner. In our family, when they were 'the flavour of the month,' we would each refer to them as,

"My son," or, "My daughter," but when they were unpopular, it would be, "What on earth has your daughter done to her hair?" or, "Your son was in a funny mood today." It's impossible to share these little nuggets with anyone else. That can never be replaced.

Entertaining friends is more difficult now. My husband would pour drinks, and talk to guests while I dished up the food. I've now resorted to giving visitors something to look at when I'm plating up (possibly a paper or a magazine) in case they venture into the kitchen and catch me salvaging the burnt carrots or mopping up gravy spilt on the floor.

I can't pretend the early days of solo entertaining were easy but I knew that if I didn't make the effort with friends, I risked never receiving invitations to dinner later on, after the initial post-funeral support. After all, if you don't make an effort with people, especially those close to you and whom you love, why should they make an effort with you?

Always eager to be thrifty, is something else that seems to have backfired. 'Special offers, two for the price of one.' All that tempting salesmanship has to be thought through carefully when catering for one. How often have I had to chuck away half a decomposing cucumber, found lurking in the back of the salad compartment?

How irresistible: a whole cucumber at 55p, when half costs 35p. One red pepper 85p, whereas three in various colours costs £1.35p. I now realise that it's a false economy. However a few of my friends have gained through my generosity, and left my company clutching half a cucumber or a selection of peppers in assorted hues.

****

Special dates
and anniversaries

There's no denying it, these are tough times, particularly during the first year. People adapt in different ways and at a different rate. Some are inconsolable for a long period whereas others appear to be in control much earlier. This might not necessarily be the case: who knows how much they might be suffering behind closed doors? They may cry privately.

Family members know it is tough and try to

ease the situation for you. Dates, such as birthdays are insignificant to those you meet on a day-to-day basis, as they are unaware of the importance to you. It is better not to draw attention to them unless it is to somebody close who would probably realise and understand.

The first year anniversary of Alan's passing wasn't good for me, but family rallied round making sure I wasn't left on my own. Now that I am able to cope, I do my own private acknowledgement of the date and try to arrange time out with a friend, more than likely including a meal somewhere. I always get a 'phone call from the family and a special friend who make sure that I am okay, but we don't make a big thing of it. It's lovely to know that they remember and care.

I have a widowed friend and we share the same wedding anniversary in September (different year) so we go out for a meal together on that date and talk about husbands and family. She hasn't been on her own as long as I have, and I feel she is still finding it a struggle. She and her husband were both good dancers and this is one of the many things she misses.

***

Many friends were kind enough to include me in their celebrations as if I were still part of a couple. This proved difficult at first as they talked about their holidays etc and said 'we' did this and 'we' we did that.

I couldn't help feeling sad and out of my comfort zone in the early days. There was no longer a 'we' in my life. I know they were completely unaware of how I felt. It was genuinely unintentional on their behalf and I'm glad they didn't know, for the conversation would have become contrived. On several occasions I made an excuse not to go out, but eventually ran out of excuses and in time the situation became easier.

****

Alone Again

Do men and women react in the same way?

People, regardless of gender or marital status react differently. There is no way that you can guess how they will be affected and it can be a surprise. Usually, if they've been a devoted couple, totally dependant and absorbed in each another and one dies, the remaining partner will not only be devastated, but they will have no idea how to rebuild their life, particularly if the organiser/

driver is the one who has passed. Where would they start? What should they do?

Occasionally the situation is reversed and the remaining widow/widower decides to prove that they can manage and they look upon it as a challenge. They were probably very happy during their marriage, letting their partner make all the decisions, but now it's their turn.

Sometimes a stormy marriage which should have ended in divorce, takes on a different aspect when one of them dies. The remaining partner is blinkered and looks upon the years spent together as a good and happy union. Thoughts change when situations change.

From my own experience and anecdotal evidence, women generally manage to cope better than men. They are usually the more domesticated, unless of course the man has been a carer and taken over the domestic duties and responsibilities which is sometimes (though much less often) the case.

A man might find it beneficial to find a cleaner if he is not familiar with housework. If funds allow, they can prove invaluable by helping to keep the home clean and tidy until he learns how to cope with the necessary chores. It is all-too easy to let standards slip when you find yourself alone with no one else to think about but yourself. But please, don't allow this to happen – what would a partner have thought about piles of unwashed dishes and carpets that haven't seen a vacuum cleaner for months?

And if he finds himself helpless in the kitchen, aside from relying on kind family and friends to drop over meals and invite him over for dinner, it's not a bad idea to invest in some basic cooking lessons. A widower I know enrolled in evening cookery classes six months after his lovely wife passed away. Not only did he learn to take care of himself better from then on, but it was a useful way of passing an hour or two a week and resulted in at least one lasting friendship by the end of the course.

Married couples normally socialise with other couples, as they have plenty in common. This often changes (more of that later). In the older age group there are more women around than men. Everywhere - clubs, holidays (solo or otherwise) classes, choirs etc - women always seem to outnumber men, which can prove disconcerting.

On the other hand, an extra man is always welcome. Some men might jump at the chance to join a group of women, while others feel daunted and pull out if they realise they will be in the minority. They will stay home and retreat into their shell along with slippers, newspapers and TV.

Come on, you guys, it's still not entirely a woman's world – find something blokey! There are plenty of societies where you can meet and enjoy a spot of male company. How about the Lions, Rotary, Probus or if you're active, the golf club?

Women are not banned at the golf club and they have their own fixtures, but there are generally more men found there than say at a keep-fit class or on a creative writing course.

Several men either join or become more involved with the Freemasons. They do plenty of charity work and it can prove to be a fulfilling pastime with a variety of events, including regular meetings followed by a meal.

Women tend to get on with life quicker and easier. Men become bored on their own and mooch around, wondering what to do. Women will pick up the 'phone, talk to a friend and say, "I'm p….d off, are you free? What shall we do?" Men let the grass grow under their feet. Women get the lawn mower out.

Alone Again

I'm not sure if this is true for men, but I know quite a few women who indulge in a 'little treat', (me included). Maybe a glass of wine when in for the evening or a chocolate or two when you arrive back? Something to look forward to is always a cheerful prospect.

Men are more likely to treat themselves to a new book, a DVD or a CD, and why not? How about a drink and a choc while you are reading the latest best seller or listening to music? It's often the most simple of things that bring the most pleasure.

****

Unfounded suspicions

It's unfair but nevertheless true: if two men are seen socialising together, apart from at the pub, Mr and Mrs Jo Public automatically assume they are gay, whereas if a pair of women are in that position (no pun intended) they are not normally given a second thought. Many innocent situations are misconstrued yet everyone has a right to choose who to spend time with, free from judgement.

Years ago my husband took our twenty-five year old daughter out for a meal and got several curious glances, especially when he called her, "Darling." She was aware of the looks they were attracting and made a point of addressing him as "Dad" at every possible opportunity (spoil sport!). It's a sad fact that in this day and age, people judge others far too quickly and often assume they're behaving inappropriately, not that it's any of their business when consenting adults are involved. At my age when out with my son, I think, "Let's keep 'em guessing!"

People read much more into everything than may exist. So often, if two people of the opposite sex and of a similar age are seen together after a bereavement, they are assumed to be an item. You can almost hear them tut, "So soon." Why can't we just live and let live nowadays? If you're bereaved and lonely and get an opportunity to pass the time with a friend of the opposite sex in the same position, don't let others deter you from doing so. We all deserve companionship and even romance if that's what the friendship leads to.

Unfounded suspicions

There is no law that says you have to mourn in black for ten years before you can be happy again.

To be honest, I have on occasions jumped to the wrong conclusion, but now I try to keep the mouth firmly zipped and my thoughts to myself. It's safer that way. I feel we all owe it to ourselves to take happiness where we can find it. After all, as we all know (especially if you're reading this book after losing your other half) no one knows what's around the corner.

****

Alone Again

Is this the answer?

Sometimes a man or woman, (especially a man if he has had a happy marriage) on the loss of a partner immediately seeks a replacement. It might be because of loneliness, not being able to cope, possibly security, or maybe they want someone to take care of them. There are many reasons. He/she might even be on the rebound and not thinking clearly.

They could, on the other hand, have had a happy marriage and enjoyed being part of a couple and are anxious to get back to that state. If the right person appears at the right time it could work out satisfactorily – but if one of them has only their own interests at heart, it could be disastrous.

The motive has to be right. Folk are very vulnerable at this time. As I've said before, it pays not to rush into anything long-term after a bereavement, although I do accept that where affairs of the heart are concerned, this is not always possible.

Some resolve after the death of a partner to never get involved with marriage or a partner again and they stick to it, but sometimes fate takes a hand and the unexpected happens and it could result in complications. What about the family? How will they react? Will they resent it and feel that someone will be taking the place of Mum/Dad? They might be suspicious of this unknown 'scrounger', Perhaps he/she might be a ruthless gold digger?

I know of someone who went on a Saga cruise two years after the passing of his wife and came back with a new 'intended.' He was over the moon but what was the reaction of his family and close friends?

Perhaps they were pleased to see him happy with a new person in his life and relieved that they were spared the responsibility if he were on his own. I'll probably never know but I do hope they received a warm reception and that the union proved to be a happy one.

If a person is intent on finding a new partner, they usually lie low for a while before setting the wheels in motion. Others, unconcerned about gossip, (and there is bound to be plenty) get cracking immediately and find the quickest and easiest way to achieve their aim. At the end of the day, as long as no one is getting hurt deliberately,

Alone Again

there are no wrongs and rights about finding love again after a bereavement and no one else's business if it happens quickly or ten years down the line.

****

Bad days

We all get them, especially early on. Hopefully as time goes on they will become less frequent and the period between them will lengthen. Odd dreams, not always pleasant, can mar sleep and often it's possible to feel the presence of the departed about the house. Several friends are convinced they have experienced contact from a loved one. They have found themselves in conversation with them and are reassured that they have found peace and happiness.

Things can be going well, then, like a dice you are thrown. For some reason, something crops up or maybe someone says something that triggers off a memory and you are back to square one. It's a strange game with only you as a competitor, but you can eventually get to the top and stay there, providing you have enough determination.

Although I have written to them trying to change it, on several occasions, the demand for water rates still comes through the post addressed to Mr and Mrs. At first I was upset, but now I just find it rather annoying!

There is no shame in admitting to having a bad day. Better to do so than let people think that they have upset you in some way: that they are to blame and they don't know the reason why.

****

Being choosy

You are now in a position to be choosy and it's possible to back off from people or places and situations that you do not enjoy. If you don't feel comfortable with certain people or unhappy in certain places, they can be crossed off your list. They might be reinstated at a later date. Meanwhile, whatever you enjoy and find fulfilling should be encouraged on a regular basis and it might involve a new set of friends.

We all know people who maybe even without

realising it, leave you feeling a bit deflated after you've spent time with them. You know the ones, they always have some tale of doom and gloom to impart, the glass half empty type. You're not being selfish by choosing to avoid them at this time and instead surround yourself with people who make you feel upbeat.

Bereavement leaves you feeling lonely and sad enough as it is without the added negativity of certain situations and companions. Right now you need to muster all your strength and energy on learning to cope on your own while forging a new and satisfactory future for yourself, so within reason, do what it takes to make this happen.

At first I did my best to avoid anything that would make me sad. I chose to read light, amusing books and watch comedy films and programmes on TV instead of anything too heavy and thought provoking. Gradually, as time passed, more serious material crept in without my being aware. Nevertheless, writing this has been a disturbing experience and one that I have no intention of repeating.

****

Alone Again

Family, friends
and cronies

Family and friends are one hundred percent important in life, especially when you are on your own.

Depending on your age group, you may be blessed with grandchildren who are the most wonderful distraction. There is always something interesting happening in a family but of course, they are a younger generation so what might interest them may not interest you.

Alone Again

With modern technology, I have on occasion felt left out and it seemed as if we lived on different planets. It's all the new gadgetry. I have a mobile 'phone which I can use for texting, or for an emergency phone call, but nowadays they are geared up to take photographs, make a cup of coffee, or tell you the cost of a postage stamp in Botswana.

My 'phone is not permanently switched on and I've had several lectures about this. Okay, so I'm a Taurus and therefore stubborn. I find it very antisocial if a smart phone is constantly in use when out for a special occasion. Why can't it be left home so that people can enjoy each others company and talk? However, I do appreciate that while I may not always agree with or understand my wonderful grandchildren, I wouldn't be without them and I cherish the times we spend together. They definitely make me feel a little less alone.

Sometimes we meet folk who are so obstinate, that whatever is suggested, they will automatically refuse. They might appear to take notice but have no intention of trying out anything new, even though it would help them considerably. On the other hand, perhaps they have their own idea of what will help them when they are emotionally ready.

The kids have pocket sized electronic toys, and at home they have a Wii. Having been invited by my Grandson to "Come upstairs and take a look at my Wii," I was quite relieved to discover that it was an attachment to the computer. At least it solves birthday and Christmas presents. The latest game is always acceptable.

Grandchildren never realise how much they can brighten a miserable day. They don't have to put on an act, as their interest and enthusiasm is spontaneous and they always have so much to tell you. I often wonder what Alan would think of our grandchildren. He'd be pretty darned proud, I am certain.

Friends can change, especially those that you have had during your marriage, it's that 'couples thing' again. Three can sometimes prove difficult. I've felt uncomfortable in the company of a few couples that we went out with when in a foursome and they probably felt the same. Perhaps we all tried too hard? I've been on holiday with two different couples and it's been most successful – no problems or awkwardness.

One couple that I have known for years, who were a great support to me with their friendship, are now in a similar situation. Sadly one of them died recently and I do so hope that the widower will manage to get his life back together again.

As mentioned earlier, there are many single women who seem to find like-minded folk. This was probably the start of 'Ladies who lunch.' My friends (who I refer to as cronies) are happy to meet up and dine at any time of the day. We tend to eat too much, drink too much and our humour can be naughty at times. These folk are invaluable for raising the spirits in all senses of the word.

We've all had sadness in our lives, but it is left behind when we get together. We go out and have plenty of laughs and return home feeling much better for it. We take it in turn to book tickets and venues and also to drive. It becomes complicated fixing a day when everyone is free, and it doesn't always happen. It's just one of those things where nobody gets upset if they can't make it. It's a case of 'better luck next time.'

Whoever is driving is treated to a drink by the passengers as a thank you but one drink only as it would be horrendous if any of us happened to be caught over the limit.

Alone Again

Friends are vital as they play such a huge part in our lives and we are fortunate if we have chosen well. Everyone is a cog in the wheel of life. Those who have gone before us have given their contribution. We who are left haven't finished yet. There is still something for us to do, and I firmly believe that every single person is here for a reason.

Now you're bereaved, don't make the mistake of shutting yourself away from your friends, claiming you can cope on your own. Accept all hands of friendship, even from people you've not seen for a while who may reach out when they hear the sad news. Never underestimate how important our friends are and remember, one day they may need you to be there for them.

****

Miscellaneous

There are a few incidental things that I have yet to mention. This may sound silly, especially to men, but a cuddly toy can be of comfort to some (as you will read about shortly when you reach Goliath). Okay, so you think that's nonsense. You've probably decided that I'm one act short of an opera, anyhow, here goes. No doubt the following will confirm what you've already thought.

People will talk to their dog, cat or canary and not get a reply, but a toy? It is said that talking to yourself is the first sign of madness, but you can get away with it providing it is a pet, so why not a toy? When you are having a wobbly, you could kick the living daylights out of a toy, but I don't suggest you try it with a dog!

Remember it's important to take care of your appearance and personal hygiene. Apart from the obvious, clean underwear, hosiery etc, don't forget a quick glance in the mirror in case that full English breakfast has manifested itself down the front of your outfit.

There is nobody to check up, so do make sure. You'll feel so much better and confident when you know that you are looking up to scratch, although that might not be the best turn of phrase!

A visit to the hairdresser is always uplifting and bucks me up no end. Men don't share this quirk but hopefully they will frequent the barber's shop from time to time to prevent emulating Rip Van Winkle.

Music can help the healing process. It will relax and sooth, exhilarate and stir. It offers an excellent antidote to stress and tension and aids a variety of emotions.

Talking books are another popular choice, and many listen while preparing a meal or doing chores. They can also induce sleep.

Apart from lending books, a library is a useful place to go for information, borrowing CDs, and possibly DVDs. This can be a welcome alternative to an evening watching some rubbish on TV.

The time factor is the biggest contributor in moving on. Some people take much longer than others, and those who appear the most upset are not necessarily the ones with the strongest feelings.

The way grief is shown doesn't measure the depth of feeling. Many with the deepest feelings manage to quietly and unobtrusively get on with life, but remain controlled.

With some, there comes a time when they have to make a conscious decision to take charge. Perhaps they eventually get the message, 'I can't go on, like this,' and resolve to turn an existence into a different, but satisfying future.

There are still situations that I would rather avoid, for instance a party where everyone is a couple and I feel like a blackberry in a strawberry punnet. I've already mentioned this.

I still don't like dining out alone. Sometimes, when it is inevitable, I will take a book or magazine. I don't enjoy going to the theatre or a concert on my own, yet for some reason I'm quite happy to see a film.

****

Goliath

Many years ago, as an anniversary present I gave my husband a toy gorilla. We called him Goliath. He had an inscrutable face and our son, Russ, always said he looked like Dad on a bad day.

We had a lot of fun with this addition to the family and made up all sorts of stories about him. He would go down to the pub every evening and would pinch our car, which he drove like a maniac. He would return home late, usually the worse for wear. Each of us would try to outdo the other with outrageous tales.

One morning when my husband was about to have a shower, I said,

"You can't go in there!"

"Why not?"

"Because Goliath's in there."

"Well, he'd better hurry up."

All silly stuff and complete nonsense, but we had many a good laugh.

Goliath doesn't lead such an adventurous life now, although he goes to bed with me each night. It's somehow reassuring to reach out and grab his paw when having a bad night.

****

Looking on the bright side

Make an attempt to acknowledge all the good things that are still in your life and do your best to enjoy them to the full.

Hopefully we all have commitments to keep us occupied, but now you are free to decide what you want to do without having to consider anyone else.

I have probably become a little selfish, for I can watch whatever I like on the TV, go to bed whenever I wish, and have a lie in if I chose. This is not such a good idea as someone will no doubt pop around unexpectedly and you will be caught out, which is highly embarrassing!

Whenever anything is mislaid nowadays, or the light left on overnight, there is nobody to blame except myself. I've left the front door unlocked on a few occasions and have to take sole responsibility.

If the choir is planning a trip abroad and organisers want to know how many would be interested, I am the first to raise my hand, I will be free. There is nobody else to take into consideration.

Coming to the end of this book is a great relief, as I do not normally write this sort of thing, but I have felt a driving force compelling me to do so.

***

Sometime ago I wrote a play in rhyme called *A Lifetime Together*, which was about two people who met and married and it parallels their life every five years. It was sad at the end, but I could cope with that, as I was living the characters and it wasn't personal.

This is different. Never has anything affected me as much and completely taken over my life: so many sleepless nights.

Since starting to write this I couldn't wait to finish so that I could, once again, pack away all those unsettling feelings back where they belong.

Hopefully, when I type those magic words THE END, I'll be able to switch off, open the window and let the sunshine in.

It will be worth the emotional disturbance, if anybody out there can find a shred of hope, help, comfort or peace within these pages.

THE END

Alone Again

A few years ago

I wrote *Alone Again* some time ago. Since then many more friends and acquaintances have joined the 'single' fraternity.

How many times have we been told that time heals? After so long, I have to admit that it's true. It doesn't restore, but it offers compensation. The birds still sing and the sun still shines (although not every day). I am able to laugh and enjoy myself without feeling guilty, yet I often think, 'He would have loved that.'

Things change all the time. You can't help wondering what he/she would think of the kids, the new housing estate nearby, the supermarket that's popped up down the road. What would their opinion be on the latest world crisis? If one of the grandchildren had a tattoo? What would they have thought of modern technology?

I know that my husband would have been delighted if my rambling jottings helped someone and chuffed that he was the instigator.

****

Useful contacts

Bereavement Advice Centre
Tel: 0800 634 9494 (Mon- Fri 9am-5pm)
Advice and information concerning a death:
Freephone Tel: 0800 634 9494

British Association for Counselling & Psychotherapy
Publishes a 'Find a therapist' directory to help you find a therapist in your local area.
www.bacp.co.uk

Citizens Advice Bureau
Charity providing practical and legal advice on various matters.
www.citizensadvice.org.uk for your local CAB

Cruse Bereavement Care
Free enquiry line Tel: 0800 144 8316
Helpline Tel: 0808 808 1677
www.cruse.org.uk

The Lions
Specialise in projects of initiative with helping
those in need.
Email: enquiries@lionsclubs.co
Tel: 0845 833 9502

Probus
For retired or semi-retired business or professional
people although membership is not restricted to
these two groups.
Tel: 0845 230 7720
www.probusworld.com

Rotary

Local action groups where friends and neighbours join leaders to create lasting changes. Women are welcome in many clubs, but may chose to join The Inner Wheel groups which have similar aims.

Tel: 01789 765 411

www.rotary.org

The Samaritans

Free call any time (UK) Tel: 116 123

www.samaritans.org

****

Also by Dawn Cawley

The Old Fart's Guide to Survival
By Dawn Cawley

Dawn Cawley, a paid-up member of The Old Fart's Club, certainly isn't ready to be put out to pasture just yet and shares her tips and observations on life in the slow lane.

From dealing with modern technology and grandkids, to old friendships and going deaf, this quirky and humorous take on later life, is a must-have survival guide for all the Old Farts who aim to grow old(er) disgracefully!

£4.99 (paperback)

Also available from Splendid Publications

**Daniel, My Son -
A Father's Powerful Account Of His Son's
Cancer Journey**
By David Thomas

Daniel was just 17, rich of talent and full of dreams, when he received the devastating news that he had bone cancer all over his body. In pain and facing horrific treatment, his chances were slim. But Daniel refused to give up on life and studied Classics at Oxford, played with the BBC Symphony Orchestra, line-judged at Wimbledon and was chosen to carry the Olympic Torch. Meanwhile his heartbroken parents scoured the world for a cure and learnt to navigate the medical maze. Their mission was to create hope – for Daniel, themselves and all those facing the same nightmare: a child with cancer. This is a father's powerful story of his love for his son and humankind's overriding need for hope.

£7.99 (paperback)

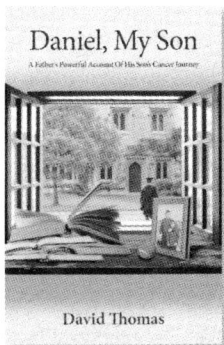

Happily Ever After...? An Essential Guide To Successful Relationships
By Janet Clegg and Hilary Browne-Wilkinson

Congratulations, you've fallen in love and from now on shouldn't it be 'happily ever after?' Sorry, falling in the love is the easy bit! With all the stresses and strains of modern life it's becoming increasingly difficult to sustain happy and loving relationships. In the UK alone nearly half of all marriages end in divorce and countless long-term partnerships fail every day.

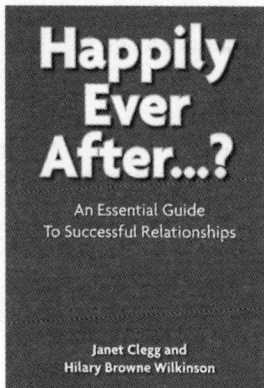

Happily Ever After...?

An Essential Guide
To Successful Relationships

Janet Clegg and
Hilary Browne Wilkinson

In Happily Ever After...? former London divorce lawyers, Janet Clegg and Hilary Browne Wilkinson, set out the vital relationship questions we should all be asking ourselves to stop us falling into the common traps which can derail even the most loving of couples.

So, if you've found the love of your life and are about to embark on a long-term relationship, or even if you've been married or in a partnership for years, this no-nonsense practical handbook, packed with easy to follow advice and examples, can help you to look forward to a happier and loving future together.

£7.99 (paperback)

William and Kate's Britain - An Insider's Guide to the haunts of the Duke and Duchess of Cambridge
By Claudia Joseph

Britain is an island with a rich cultural heritage, which dates back to the Roman era: it is a land of pubs and football; rock music and opera; historic palaces and village churches; breath-taking scenery and ancient monuments. That's not to mention its spectacular pageantry – the royal wedding ceremony at St Paul's Cathedral and the Queen's Diamond Jubilee celebrations were beamed to billions around the world. Now, in a unique guide to the British Isles, royal author Claudia Joseph goes behind the scenes – and reveals the secrets – of William and Kate's Britain.

£9.99 (paperback)

How to Survive Divorce
By Anthea Turner

TV presenter Anthea Turner was devastated when her husband Grant Bovey cheated on her with a woman young enough to be his daughter. Although both she and Grant had left their previous partners for each other, Anthea was convinced they had both learned from their mistakes and were destined to grow old together. Heartbroken, she filed for divorce.

How to Survive Divorce is Anthea's candid take on the emotional toll the end of her marriage took on her well-being and how she eventually came out of the ordeal, a stronger, more confident woman. Open and honest, she pulls no punches as she describes falling apart in the months after the split and turning to her friends, family and professionals to help her through her darkest days.

This is a book which has been carefully researched and written by the star and is full of helpful tips and real-life case studies. How to Survive Divorce aims to offer women who find themselves facing divorce – whether or not from choice – practical help and guidance in navigating what can be a legal and emotional minefield. From choosing the right solicitor to getting back in the dating game, this is a must-have guide on how to survive divorce and come out the other side.

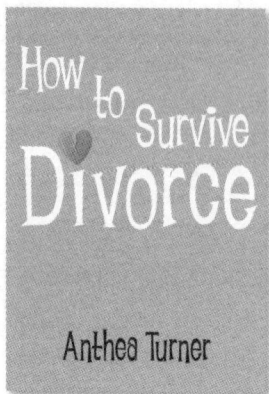

£9.99 (paperback)

108

How to Dress Like a Princess
By Claudia Joseph

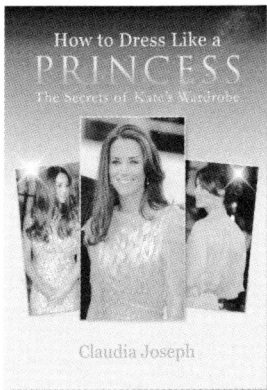

Britain is one of the fashion capitals of the world, with a rich heritage of avant-garde designers: the name Mary Quant encapsulated the swinging sixties; Vivienne Westwood symbolised punk and is now - almost - a national treasure and the late Alexander McQueen left an extraordinary legacy in his tragically short life. Yet, there is another, equally important, dress code in our country - and its ambassador is the Duchess of Cambridge.

Now, as she investigates the rules for dressing for the social season, fashion journalist and Royal author Claudia Joseph unveils the secrets of Kate's wardrobe.

£12.99 (paperback)

Order online at:
www.splendidpublications.co.uk